THE
Byzantine
EMPIRE

by Jenny Fretland VanVoorst

Content Adviser:
Richard Greenfield, PhD
Professor of History
Queen's University, Kingston, Ontario

COMPASS POINT BOOKS
a capstone imprint

Compass Point Books
1710 Roe Crest Drive
North Mankato, MN 56003
www.capstonepub.com

Managing Editor: Catherine Neitge
Designers: Heidi Thompson and Lori Bye
Media Researcher: Eric Gohl
Library Consultant: Kathleen Baxter
Production Specialist: Laura Manthe

Image Credits
Bridgeman Art Library: Gift of Helen Stathatos, 25, Giraudon, 14, Photo © AISA, 41; Corbis:
8, The Art Archive/Alfredo Dagli Orti, 17, 33, Bettmann, 15, Burstein Collection, 13, Richard T.
Nowitz, 18; Getty Images: Hulton Archive, 19, 21; iStockphoto: faraways, cover (top right), frac-
tal, cover (bottom right); Newscom: akg-images, 4, 7, 12, 20, 26, akg-images/Cameraphoto, 36,
akg-images/Maurice Babey, 43, Design Pics, 5, Getty Images/AFP/HO, 24, Oronoz/Album, 42,
World History Archive, 37; Shutterstock: Artur Bogacki, 32, Dr. Saqib-ul-Hasan, 38, imagestalk,
9, jejim, 28, John Copland, 22, Luciano Mortula, 30, mountainpix, 29, 31, 34, Nikolay Stefanov
Dimitrov, cover (bottom left), Pavle Marjanovic, 11, 16, 40

Design Elements: Shutterstock: LeshaBu, MADDRAT, renew studio

Library of Congress Cataloging-in-Publication Data
  VanVoorst, Jennifer, 1972–
The Byzantine Empire / by Jenny Fretland VanVoorst.
    p. cm.
Includes bibliographical references and index.
ISBN 978-0-7565-4565-9 (library binding)
ISBN 978-0-7565-4586-4 (paperback)
ISBN 978-0-7565-4627-4 (ebook PDF)
1. Byzantine Empire—Civilization—Juvenile literature. I. Title.
DF552.V265 2013
949.5'02—dc23   2012001994

Editor's Note: Compass Point Books uses new abbreviations to
distinguish time periods. For ancient times, instead of BC, we
use BCE, which means before the common era. BC means before
Christ. Similarly, we use CE, which means in the common era,
instead of AD. The abbreviation AD stands for the Latin phrase
anno Domini, which means in the year of our Lord, referring to Jesus Christ.

Printed in the United States of America in Stevens Point, Wisconsin.
032012   006678WZF12

Table of CONTENTS

Chapter 1

Rome Moves East

Black smoke mingled with the dust of crushed stone as cannonballs erupted through the city walls. The double walls of Constantinople had held strong for most of the past 1,000 years, but the empire had weakened over the centuries.

Emperor Constantine XI wondered whether this would be

the final siege. The Ottoman Turks had been bombarding the city for nearly two months, and its citizens, trapped behind the walls, were sick and starving. But if Constantinople were to fall, it would mean the end of the empire. It would mean that the dream of Constantine I, the first emperor of Byzantium, was not fulfilled. His dream of a Christian empire bridging East and West was over.

As ball after ball broke through the walls and enemy soldiers streamed through, Constantine XI, the 81st emperor of this once vast empire, again rallied his troops against the Ottoman Turks. There was much more than just the city at stake. One of the last surviving direct links to the ancient world was under attack.

When the Byzantine Empire fell to the Ottoman Turks in 1453, it was the end of an important but poorly recognized period of world history. When we think of the time period from the fourth century through the 15th century, we usually think of western Europe struggling in the Dark Ages. The Roman Empire, which flourished at the beginning of the first century, had preserved and expanded upon the knowledge and culture of the ancients. But when invading Germanic tribes ended its reign, the

The Ottoman Turks conquered Constantinople in 1453 (left).
Constantine XI (above) was the last Byzantine emperor.

light of knowledge dimmed for 1,000 years. At least that is the story commonly known. But it is not entirely true.

In actuality, the Roman Empire didn't collapse entirely. It moved east, where it nurtured religion, centralized government and law, and developed music, art, philosophy, mathematics, and other areas of scholarship. While western Europe was often in the dark, in the East the light continued to shine.

The story of the rise of Byzantium starts with the decline in importance of the city of Rome. In 293 CE, facing the invading Germanic hordes, the rulers of the Roman Empire decided to change the way the empire was governed. Instead of being ruled from Rome by a single emperor, the empire was divided into eastern and western regions, each to be governed by a separate emperor who in turn had help from a deputy emperor.

Diocletian, who led the empire from 284 to 305, was the ruler of the eastern territories and governed from a city in what today is Turkey. When he voluntarily retired in 305, and the western emperor died the following year, this scheme collapsed. Constantine, son of the former emperor of the West, emerged as the strongest claimant to power. Over the next 18 years, he managed to defeat the other rulers and take control of the entire empire.

Like Diocletian, Constantine decided to live in the eastern part of the Roman world. He set about finding a new capital city—a city that would work more effectively than old Rome in the empire he was determined to rebuild and transform. He chose a city named Byzantium.

A Greek named Byzas had founded Byzantium in the mid-600s BCE. The Delphic Oracle, the seer of Greek legend, had guided him to establish the city. About 1,000 years later, Constantine was supposedly guided by a dream to choose the location for his new capital. He renamed the city Constantinople, which means "City of Constantine." It was also known as New Rome.

The site had many features that made it an attractive capital and center of trade. Located on a peninsula between the Aegean Sea and the Black Sea, it was a

The Founding of Constantinople, an oil sketch by Peter Paul Rubens, is one of 12 on the life of Constantine by the famed 17th century painter.

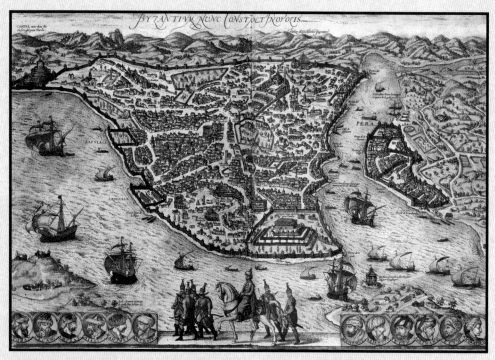

Constantinople was located on the Bosporus Strait, which connects the Black Sea to the Mediterranean Sea.

very defensible location. It was also ideally situated for commerce. It was a crossroads for trade routes between Europe and Asia, and linked African routes.

Because of its strategic location for trade, Constantinople was a very cosmopolitan city, and it grew quickly. People from various parts of the world were drawn to the city and could be found mingling in its markets. But in the eastern provinces of the empire, Greek culture overlay the heritage of many ancient cultures. So Constantinople, like Byzantium before it, was at heart a Greek city. Although Latin was the official language until the sixth century, the citizens of Constantinople, as well as most of the rest of the empire, spoke Greek. But they considered themselves, as did everyone in the empire, to be Romans. It is only in modern times that the Roman Empire in the east has come to be known as the Byzantine Empire.

Like the Roman Empire that preceded it, the Byzantine Empire was so large that its borders were difficult to defend. During its history of more than 1,000 years, the empire's territory included parts of 34 present-day countries in Europe, the Middle East, and North Africa. Over the centuries the empire did its best to defend itself against many invaders who wanted to gain territory or plunder the riches of Constantinople. Turks, Persians, Arabs, Bulgars, and even Christian crusaders were some of the groups waging war against the Byzantines. During that time the Byzantine borders contracted and expanded. But Byzantium grew ever smaller until 1453, when the Ottoman Turks breached the city's double walls to capture Constantinople, which at that point was nearly all that remained of the empire.

Today Constantinople is called Istanbul, and it is a thoroughly modern city in Turkey. Islam has replaced Christianity as the guiding religion. But the city is still a bridge between Europe and Asia. And because so many traditions persist from Byzantine times, it is also a bridge to the past.

Constantine's decision in the fourth century to base his empire in Byzantium has profoundly shaped

Constantine, who died in 337, was probably born in the late 280s.

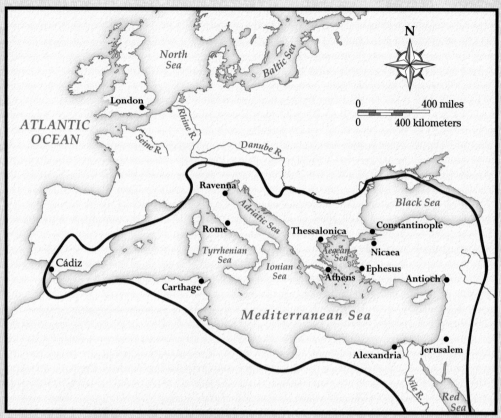

The Byzantine Empire in the mid-sixth century

our world in the 21st century. Much of what we think and believe today is founded on knowledge and ideas that came from ancient Greece. If the Byzantines had not preserved that classical knowledge—and continued the intellectual advancement—much of the knowledge would certainly have been lost. The cultural and intellectual flowering of the Renaissance in Europe might never have happened.

The Byzantine Empire is responsible for shaping our world in another way as well. This empire is responsible for the rise of Christianity. In 330, when Constantine moved his capital to the east, Christianity had a devoted but small collection of followers. In Rome and elsewhere, Christians were persecuted and even killed as entertainment in gladiatorial and animal fights. After Constantine's conversion to Christianity in 312, he gave it the same legal status as other faiths. Eventually Christianity would become the official religion of the empire and would influence all of its political dealings.

Detail of a mosaic of Constantine with a model of Constantinople

Chapter 2

An Empire of
Christ

Before the reign of Constantine, the Roman Empire was no place to be a Christian. Churches were routinely burned, and Christians were subject to all sorts of persecution and torture. They were burned at the stake, forced to take part in gladiatorial contests, and thrown to the lions for the amusement of audiences, and they suffered many other horrible fates.

In 311 Emperor Galerius gave Christians the right to

practice their religion and to rebuild their churches without interference. But Christianity was only tolerated—that is, until Constantine gained sole power in 324.

Constantine had not always been a Christian. Like most of the populace, he practiced polytheism. He worshipped such Roman deities as Jupiter, Mars, Venus, and especially Apollo, the sun god. But in 312, when he was fighting to wrest control of the empire from his co-rulers, he had a vision. According to legend, he saw a cross and heard a voice from heaven that told him, "In this sign, conquer." He adopted the Christian faith and went on to defeat his rivals and take control of the empire.

Christian martyrs (left) were thrown to the lions and other beasts in Rome. Constantine (above) was said to have seen a cross from God.

A 13th century Italian mosaic of Saint Helena and her son, Constantine; she may have influenced her son's conversion to Christianity.

During Constantine's rule, Christianity began to be actively supported. As a result, the religion flourished and spread. It also became part of the political landscape. The Byzantine Empire became a theocracy in the sense that Christian values and ideals were the foundation of the empire's political ideals and heavily entwined with its political goals. In fact, the old religious practice of polytheism—the belief in more than one god or many gods—was eventually outlawed in 392.

The emperor was believed to be the representative of God on Earth and a counterpart to Jesus Christ. He was believed to be chosen by God himself and so to rule by divine right. As such he occupied a key role not only in the affairs of state but also in the church. But the emperor could not decide matters of belief by himself, and attempts to impose his authority in other religious matters often led to controversy and conflict.

As the political and religious center of the empire, Constantinople came to be known as the New Jerusalem. The city was full of holy relics, and many of its coins had Jesus' face on them.

Part of Byzantium's political power came from the fact that the majority of its citizens held the same set of religious beliefs, something that helped to strengthen and unify the empire. Over time, most Christians came to agree upon a standard set of beliefs that were thought to be correct or "orthodox." In response to serious disagreements between various groups of Christians, a series of meetings among church leaders, known as councils, established what those beliefs were to be. The First Council of Nicaea in 325 determined such issues as the relationship of Jesus Christ to God the Father and the proper date of Easter. The Council also was responsible for writing the first part of the Nicene Creed, a Christian profession of faith that is still used in church liturgy today. Over the next 400 years, six more councils followed to clarify and codify other issues of belief.

During the 500 or so years that followed the loss of Byzantine political control in the old Roman

Three hundred bishops gathered at the First Council of Nicaea.

A church mosaic features 12th century ruler John II Comnenus and Empress Irene making offerings to the church, represented by the Virgin Mary and Jesus.

West, a number of differences developed in the practice and beliefs of Christians in these regions. Some concerned cultural issues (such as whether to use Latin or Greek in services or whether priests should be married or wear beards). Others involved matters of authority (who should be the leader of the church—the pope or the council of bishops?) and doctrine (the relation of Father, Son, and Spirit in the Holy Trinity).

By 1054 awareness of these differences had grown and the rift between East and West was formalized. The eastern church separated from the western church in a split known as the Schism, and this division hardened over the next two centuries. These two branches of Christianity persist today, with more than 1 billion people worldwide practicing Roman Catholicism, mostly in western Europe and the Americas, and as many as 300 million people practicing Orthodox Christianity, largely in eastern Europe and Russia.

Cyrillic Alphabet

With adoption of Christianity as the official religion, monks and others actively sought to convert the polytheists and spread Christianity throughout the empire. Although missionary work was never widely practiced by Byzantine Christians, it was sometimes employed beyond the empire's borders to help expand Byzantine political influence. In such circumstances a language barrier might complicate the process.

The modern Cyrillic alphabet is based on one created by a ninth century monk named Cyril who was sent to preach the Christian faith to the Slavs of central Europe. The script was adapted from written Greek, adding additional consonants and pronunciation markers for sounds not found in Greek.

The alphabet is still in use today by dozens of languages in eastern Europe and Asia, including Russian, Bulgarian, and Mongolian, as well as some native languages of Alaska.

Saints Cyril and Methodius were brothers who together served as missionaries.

Chapter 3

Intellectual Achievements

Though we primarily credit the Byzantines with preserving classical learning during the Middle Ages, they also made important intellectual and artistic contributions of their own in a number of areas.

One of the notable achievements of Byzantine society was in the area of law. The Byzantines highly valued the rule of law. When Emperor Justinian came to power in 527, one of his

primary concerns was understanding and organizing the vast body of laws the empire had inherited from the Romans. He appointed a committee to tackle this project. The result was a coherent and consistent set of laws—both old and new—called the Code of Justinian. Scholars consider this legal code to be one of the most significant accomplishments of the emperor's reign.

Justinian also wanted to use the law to uphold the teachings of Jesus Christ. He made sure his Code included new laws that improved the circumstances of traditionally powerless or disadvantaged groups, such as women, slaves, and debtors.

Not all laws in the Code of Justinian were designed to help people. Some were designed to punish. The death penalty was rarely applied, but when a criminal was executed, it was a public spectacle. Many crimes were punished with blinding or the loss of a hand, nose, or tongue.

Emperor Justinian (center left and above) ruled from 527 until his death in 565.

The Code of Justinian called for some brutal punishments by today's standards. But at the time, it was considered a humane collection of laws that could be applied fairly and without confusion.

The Byzantines were an educated, literate society, and they produced an impressive amount of literature. Although most of it was religious, there were also histories, encyclopedias, secular poetry, and books of fiction and nonfiction. Some humor writing reveals that the Byzantines had a taste for simple jokes and puns. Literary forms and writing styles could be traced back to ancient Greek models.

The printing press would not be invented until the 15th century, so books in Byzantine times were copied by hand. Usually this work was completed by ordinary scribes, but sometimes, and especially in the case of religious works, it was done by monks. They copied important manuscripts in special rooms called scriptoria. The empire had many monasteries, and they were powerful forces in Byzantine cultural life, often supported by the nobility or members of the imperial family.

In medieval western Europe, learning came to

Detail of King David's penance from a 10th century illuminated manuscript known as the *Paris Psalter*

Empress Theodora

The best-known Byzantine historian was Procopius, the court historian during the reign of Justinian I. For public consumption he wrote *Wars of Justinian* and *Buildings of Justinian*, which celebrated the emperor's achievements in battle and architecture. He also wrote a book, *Secret History*, in which he told little-known stories about the emperor's dark side and reveled in the secret scandals of Justinian's wife, Empress Theodora.

In his official accounts, Procopius paints a picture of Empress Theodora as a strong woman of great piety and political influence. But in *Secret History,* he reveals an entirely different side to the empress. He details some of her more risqué behavior, such as dancing on stage wearing nothing but a ribbon.

How much truth there is to what Procopius wrote is questionable, but it is true that Theodora had an interesting life. The daughter of the bear trainer at the Hippodrome, Theodora grew up in the shadow of the building's famed spectacles and became a stage

Theodora had a daughter, but she and Justinian had no children together.

performer. After living as the mistress to several wealthy and powerful men, she met Justinian, who had the laws changed to allow him to marry someone of her background.

As empress, Theodora was a champion for women, and her influence was important in passing many laws regarding their rights and protection. Whatever the truth of Procopius' writings, Theodora is honored as a saint by the Orthodox Church and known as a pioneer of feminism.

be associated entirely with the church and its monasteries, but in the Byzantine world this was not the case. Education, especially at higher levels, was something pursued primarily in the secular world. The Byzantines valued education, and many citizens of the empire were well educated. Many men received a good education, including members of the middle class. Some women were educated too, but not as many, nor was their education quite so good. Usually only upper-class women could read and write.

Much education was directed at enabling people to speak well in public or to work in the vast administrative system of the empire. But some Byzantines were accomplished scientists working in such fields as mathematics, astronomy, botany, or medicine.

Music is considered one of the Byzantines' chief cultural achievements. Byzantine music that remains today is exclusively religious in nature. Sacred music was written for the voice alone. Instruments such as lyres, horns, flutes, and drums were used in secular music, but they were not considered appropriate for religious use. Chants and hymns that originated during the Byzantine period are still

Byzantine mosaic from Cyrenaica, in what is now eastern Libya

used in Orthodox church services around the world. The enduring religious tradition has kept this music alive. All of the secular music has been lost to time, although echoes of it may still be heard in the folk music of Greece and Turkey.

The Byzantines' crowning achievements were in the areas of art and architecture. The Byzantines lavished much of their artistic skill on their churches. Byzantine churches were characterized by a large central dome, which made worshippers inside feel as if they could look up into heaven. The interiors were decorated with frescoes and mosaic art. Artists often covered entire walls with scenes from the Bible, as well as depicting scenes from the reigns of emperors.

The Byzantines adopted a consistent, rather stylized form of artistic representation to suggest the holiness of the subjects. These stylized human forms were also easier to create using mosaics, the Byzantines'

most famous method of artistic expression. Small squares of cut glass, stone, or other material were pressed into plaster to create elaborate pictures and designs. These mosaics, often with gold backgrounds, adorned the walls and domes of churches and palaces throughout the Byzantine Empire.

The Byzantines also created a more personal kind of art in the form of portable icons. These were religious images painted on wooden panels that were displayed not only in the churches but also in private homes, where they may have been parts of household shrines. They were often part of ceremonial processions, both religious and military.

Byzantine artists also worked with gold and gems to create beautiful containers for Constantinople's many holy relics. Called reliquaries, these containers held items of religious significance, such as bones of saints or wood that supposedly was from the cross on which Jesus was crucified.

As one might expect in a culture so centered on religion, the majority of Byzantine art that survives was made for sacred purposes. Most secular art and architecture has perished with time, although the magnificent walls of Constantinople still stand.

An icon from the 1100s, *Ladder of Divine Ascent,* features monks facing demons as they climb a ladder to Jesus.

Iconoclasm

During the 700s and 800s, there was a major conflict in Byzantine society over the role of art in worship. Icons were used to promote piety and teach the faith, but some in Byzantine society feared that using icons in worship came dangerously close to idolatry, the worshiping of images. They also were concerned that icons emphasized the human aspects of Jesus Christ rather than the divine. Emperor Leo III believed the latter, and in 730 he banned all icons and other religious art. Many beautiful mosaics, frescoes, and icons were destroyed. Called iconoclasm, from the Greek meaning "image breaking," this policy was put in place and overturned by various emperors for more than a century.

Iconoclasm came to an end in 843, and icons have played a central role in Orthodox Christian worship ever since. Today the word is often used to refer to the challenging of convention. People who question or attack beliefs or institutions are known as iconoclasts.

A 16th century icon, *The Restoration of the Icons,* celebrates the end of iconoclasm.

Chapter 4

Town and Country

Life in the Byzantine Empire differed greatly based on whether an individual lived in the city or the country and based on personal wealth and social standing.

Life in Constantinople was very cosmopolitan for its time. Because the city was the administrative center of the empire and important to trade, residents of Constantinople and visitors were ethnically and culturally diverse. The docks were crowded with all sorts of boats, while the streets teemed with a variety of people, including Scandinavians, Egyptians, North Africans, and Persians. Because of its role as a meeting place between East and West, Constantinople dominated the world market. Byzantine merchants and other traders imported products from as far away as Iceland, Ethiopia, northern Russia, Sri Lanka, and China. Shops displayed luxury goods such as silks, gold jewelry, ivory carvings, fine leather, perfumes, decorative glass, and ceramics. The city was the center of almost all commerce, and it prospered by receiving, refining, and re-exporting the goods that passed through its markets.

Constantinople grew quickly. The city had double walls and moats and was one of the best-fortified cities in the world at the time. Constantinople reached its cultural and economic peak in the sixth century under Emperor Justinian I. At this time the population of the city is estimated to have been about 500,000.

The life of the city centered on three great structures or groups of buildings—the Hippodrome, the Hagia Sophia, and the Great Palace. The buildings represented the three main elements of the Byzantine world: the people, the church, and the emperor. The buildings enclosed the main public square, the Augustaeum.

The Hippodrome was an enormous open-air arena used for

A 1493 German woodcut of Constantinople

An ancient obelisk, which had been shipped from Egypt, was placed in the Hippodrome by Emperor Theodosius I in 390.

public entertainment such as chariot races, armed combat, and wild animal shows. It was also where criminals were publicly punished, and the public turned out in droves to see them paraded, beaten, maimed, or killed. Measuring 1,477 feet (450 meters) long by 427 feet (130 m) wide, the Hippodrome could seat more than 60,000 spectators. A typical day at the arena might include as many as 25 chariot races, with performances by acrobats, jugglers, musicians, and dancers between events. Events at the Hippodrome were the city's most popular entertainment.

The church of Hagia Sophia, Greek for "Holy Wisdom," was another cornerstone of Constantinople. The great building that still stands today is the third church of that name constructed on the site.

The Nika Riots

The Byzantines were avid sports fans, and thousands attended chariot races at the Hippodrome. The teams of charioteers were named after the colors they wore, blue and green, and each team was associated with a political party. In 532 tension was high over dissatisfaction with the emperor. The two groups were feeling particularly hostile, both against each other and against the government in general.

Tensions came to a head when the crowd in the Hippodrome got out of control and went on a five-day rampage. The crowd demanded that the emperor Justinian be replaced. Shouting "Nika!" (the word meaning "Win!" that they used to cheer on the charioteers) they burned and destroyed much of the city, including the old church of Hagia Sophia. Emperor Justinian called in the military to put down the uprising. He ended the riots and weakened the power of the Blues and Greens, but his victory came at great cost. He regained control of his empire, but 30,000 lives were lost in the Hippodrome in the process.

Empress Theodora (center) advised her husband, Justinian, to attack the rioters, which he did.

The beautiful Hagia Sophia has served as a museum since 1935.

The first church was initially built by Constantine's son in 360, but it was destroyed in 404 during a period of violent rioting. The second church also burned, during the Nika revolt in 532. But by 537 it had been magnificently rebuilt by architects employed by Justinian. Although its dome collapsed during an earthquake in 558, it was restored and made larger and stronger than ever. Today, more than 1,400 years after its construction, the church of Hagia Sophia is still believed by many to be one of the most beautiful buildings in the world. It is a spectacular example of Byzantine architecture, with a splendid dome that rises to 160 feet (49 m). Its vast interior was filled with elaborate mosaics and decorations made of colored marbles, stone, and gold. Byzantium's most important ceremonies took place inside Hagia Sophia and people felt that visiting it was like experiencing heaven on Earth.

Next to Hagia Sophia and across the Augustaeum from the Hippodrome was the Great Palace. It was a vast complex of buildings containing living quarters, dining halls, reception rooms, churches, and recreational spaces. It also had libraries, a polo ground, gardens, a swimming pool, and prisons. Apart from a few ruined walls none of these building still stands, but in Byzantine times the palace complex was central to the empire. It functioned not only as the emperor's residence but also as the hub of the administration that ran the Byzantine world. It included offices, meeting rooms, the mint, garrisons, armories and all kinds of workshops.

In addition to its grand churches and palaces, Constantinople benefitted from many innovations that were unknown in western Europe for most of this period. For example, the city's water came in by means of aqueducts from outlying hills and was stored in large underground cisterns. There

A mosaic of a young man playing hoops from the remains of the Great Palace

A surviving section of the 4th century Valens Aqueduct stands tall in Istanbul.

was even a sewage system. Many regulations governed building, trade, and safety matters.

Constantinople was the glittering jewel in the crown of Byzantium, but other significant towns and cities flourished at various times. Among them were Alexandria, Antioch, Corinth, Ephesus, Mistra, Philadelphia, Thessaloniki, and Trebizond, many of which were along the coasts.

Most of what we know about the Byzantine Empire comes from writers who lived in the cities, but most people in the empire lived close to the land. The economic life of rural Byzantium was based on agriculture, craft, and commerce. Citizens lived in small villages and owned fields, vineyards, or orchards that they worked themselves or leased to tenants. They prized self-sufficiency, and families were largely able to provide for their own needs. They grew fruit and vegetables, milled grain, wove cloth, made baskets, and created candles. When they could, they sold some of their handicrafts in the town market to make extra money for the family. And if they could afford it, they kept a few animals for meat and dairy foods and to do the heavy work in the fields. But owning land was the primary source of wealth, and the major rural landowners, whether secular lords, military leaders, or bishops and abbots in the church, were key players in society.

Detail from an early 11th century manuscript

Chapter 5

Expansion and Contraction

Although the Byzantine Empire was a stable state compared with much of western Europe during the Middle Ages, its borders expanded and contracted throughout its history as territory was gained and lost. The empire came into existence because of the threat to the western Roman Empire that was posed by invading Germanic tribes. Over the next 1,000 years, invaders from Persia, the Arab world, Italy, Bulgaria, central Asia, and elsewhere sought to gain control of parts of the empire for themselves. Constantinople was a particular prize, given its great wealth and strategic location for trade.

In the sixth and early seventh centuries, with political power in western Europe almost entirely lost, the empire's main foe was the Persians. Battles were fought for 100 years, with each side alternately winning and losing. But just when it seemed the Byzantines were finally victorious, a new and even stronger opponent appeared. After the prophet Mohammed died in 632, Arab armies looked to expand the Islamic world in every direction. The Byzantine Empire lost all its territory in what today are Syria, Palestine, and Egypt. The area they had fought over with Persia came under the control of Muslim Arabs as well.

The empire also faced many invaders from eastern Europe and the grassy plains of central Asia. Slavic peoples moved into the Balkans with their Bulgar overlords from the sixth century and fought against the Byzantine Empire. By 1018, however, they were finally defeated and had been converted to Christianity. Their territory was absorbed into the empire. Later in that century, Normans from northern France defeated the Byzantines to take territory in southern Italy, while the Seljuq Turks took control of much of what is Turkey today.

In 1095 Emperor Alexius I asked the pope, Urban II, for help in driving off the Muslim Seljuq Turks. His request led to the beginning of the Crusades, a series of expeditions sent by the

A mosaic of a Byzantine warrior from Constantinople's Great Palace

Roman Catholic Church over the next 200 years to recapture the Holy Lands in the Middle East, including the holy city of Jerusalem, from the Muslims.

The expedition now known as the Fourth Crusade was launched in 1202. Instead of taking the Holy Land, however, the crusaders ended up besieging Constantinople. Two years later, in 1204, they had captured the city, looted its treasures, destroyed many of its buildings, and set up their own version of the empire in some former Byzantine territories. These areas were now ruled by European lords. Although the western powers could not maintain their hold on these territories, and the Byzantines recovered Constantinople in 1261,

Detail from Tinoretto's ca. 1580 painting, *The Conquest of Constantinople, 1204*

this was a blow from which the empire never fully recovered.

But it wasn't long before another powerful threat reared its head, one that would be the greatest—and last. The Ottomans, another Muslim Turkish people, gained power during the 1300s and gradually took over the remaining shreds of the Byzantine Empire. The empire was wracked by almost constant civil wars, and by 1400 little of the empire was left besides Constantinople. But still the Byzantines clung to power in their capital. In 1453, however, the Ottomans had the city surrounded by land and sea and were ready to make their final assault. They bombarded Constantinople's great double walls using their newly invented cannons. The citizens continued to resist, despite being weakened and much reduced in number by disease and starvation. But after nearly two

Ottoman Sultan Mehmed II was only 21 when his armies conquered Constantinople.

months of constant bombardment, the Ottomans finally breached the city walls.

With Constantinople in their hands they quickly began establishing

The Blue Mosque, named for the 20,000 blue tiles that line its ceiling, dominates the skyline of modern Istanbul.

a new empire on the ruins of the old. They transformed the Christian city to suit their Muslim faith. Hagia Sophia and many other churches were converted to mosques. A great new mosque, the Blue Mosque, was built on the ruins of the old imperial palace, while the sultan built himself a new palace, today called Topkapi Palace. Constantinople, renamed Istanbul—the "city of Islam"— became the capital of a vast new empire stretching from southeastern Europe through the Near East to North Africa. The Ottoman Empire ruled for nearly 500 years, until the country of Turkey was formed from its wreckage in 1923. Today, with a population close to 14 million, Istanbul is the largest city in Turkey and still an important bridge between East and West.

Emperor	Period of Rule	Known For
Diocletian	284–305	Divided Roman Empire into two parts, planting the seed of the Byzantine Empire
Constantine I	306–337	Made Christianity the foundation on which the Byzantine Empire was built
Julian	361–363	Rejected Christianity and attempted to return the empire to its polytheistic roots
Zeno	474–475; 476–491	Influential in ending a religious controversy; was emperor at the fall of the Western Roman Empire
Justinian	527–565	Created the Code of Justinian, rewriting and codifying the laws of the empire
Heraclius	610–641	Established Greek as the empire's official language; was emperor at the birth of Islam
Irene	797–802	Influential in restoring icons to Orthodox religious practice
Basil I	867–886	Capable emperor whose reign was marked by an artistic renaissance
Basil II	976–1025	Conquered Bulgaria and expanded the empire's eastern frontier
Alexius I	1081–1118	Stabilized the empire after a period of political crisis
Michael VIII	1259–1282	Recovered Constantinople and founded the last great Byzantine dynasty
Constantine XI	1449–1453	Final ruler of the Byzantine Empire

Chapter 6

Our Byzantine Heritage

The Byzantine Empire played a vital role in shaping the course of history and culture in both the East and the West. Constantine had established Christianity as a dominant religious force. Throughout the centuries when European

society and culture was in disorder, the Byzantine Empire preserved the faith as the foundation of its political ideals and kept intellectual life vigorous. In doing so, it blocked Islam from spreading into Europe. Had Islam spread, it would have dramatically changed the future for Europe and for the New World, which was yet to be revealed to Europeans.

It is interesting to wonder how the western world might be different today had Byzantium not existed or survived

Byzantine art spans the centuries: an 11th century mosaic in the Hagia Sophia (left) and a 15th century depiction of Constantinople (above)

A rare 12th century illustrated manuscript, the *Madrid Skylitzes*, named after its author John Skylitzes, covers nearly 200 years of Byzantine history.

for more than 1,000 years. How might things be different today had missionaries not spread the growing faith and monasteries not preserved the religious rituals of Orthodox Christianity? And what might have happened had the Byzantines not preserved the intellectual heritage of the Greeks? What knowledge might have been lost, and how would that have changed the way we think today? The Byzantines' preservation of classical knowledge contributed significantly to the flourishing of culture that was the Renaissance.

The Byzantine Empire kept the

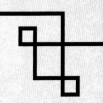

Pearls and gems decorate a golden 10th century book of the gospels.

life of ancient Greece and Rome—
transformed and re-energized by
the Christian faith—shining while
western Europe struggled through
the Dark Ages. So much of what
the West is today comes from the
fact that for 1,000 years in the East
there was a golden empire now
known as Byzantium.

Timeline

658 BCE	Byzantium is founded by Greek colonists
293 CE	Diocletian reorganizes the Roman Empire
303–311	Church burnings, ordered by Emperor Diocletian and continued by his successor, mark the last of the great anti-Christian persecutions
306	Constantine I becomes co-emperor
312	Constantine converts to Christianity
324	Constantine becomes the sole emperor and moves the capital to Byzantium
325	First ecumenical council, held at Nicaea, defines the Orthodox Christian faith
330	Byzantium, renamed Constantinople, is proclaimed capital of the Roman Empire
413-439	Theodosius II extends and fortifies the city walls
476	Rome falls to the Ostrogoths; the western part of the Roman Empire ends
527–565	Justinian I rules during the golden age of the empire
529	Justinian compiles a legal code
537	Hagia Sophia, in Constantinople, is rebuilt
726-842	Period of iconoclasm (except the years 780–813)
1054	The Schism—the Orthodox Church officially breaks with the Church of Rome
1095	Pope Urban II calls the First Crusade
1202-1204	Crusaders capture and sack Constantinople during the Fourth Crusade
1204-1261	Latin rulers govern Constantinople
1261	Byzantine rule is restored in Constantinople
1453	Constantinople falls to the Ottoman Turks, ending the Byzantine Empire

Glossary

cosmopolitan—familiar with and at ease in many cultures

crusades—military expeditions undertaken by European Christians from 1095 to 1291 to recover Palestine from the Muslims

fresco—kind of mural painting in which paint is applied to a special layer of plaster while it is damp

icon—religious image, usually painted on a wooden panel

iconoclasm—literally "image breaking;" a movement of the eighth and ninth centuries against the use of icons

monastery—place where monks live and work

mosaic—picture or design made by fitting together bits of stone, glass, or tile of various colors and cementing them in place

orthodox—conforming to established religious doctrine

piety—the quality of being religious or reverent

polytheism—belief in more than one god, or in many gods

relic—object that belonged to a holy person and is highly valued

reliquaries—containers for holding relics

schism—formal division

secular—not religious

theocracy—form of government in which God is recognized as the civil ruler and church authorities interpret laws

Select Bibliography

Angold, Michael. *Byzantium: The Bridge From Antiquity to the Middle Ages.*
New York: St. Martin's Press, 2001.

Brownworth, Lars. *Lost to the West: The Forgotten Byzantine Empire That Rescued Western Civilization.* New York: Crown Publishers, 2009.

Gregory, Timothy. *A History of Byzantium.*
Chichester, U.K.: Wiley-Blackwell, 2010.

Haldon, John. *Byzantium at War.* Oxford, U.K.: Osprey Publishing, 2002.

Harris, Jonathan. *Byzantium and the Crusades.*
New York: Hambledon and London, 2003.

Herrin, Judith. *Byzantium: The Surprising Life of a Medieval Empire.*
Princeton, N.J.: Princeton University Press, 2007.

Mango, Cyril, Ed. *The Oxford History of Byzantium.*
Oxford, U.K.: Oxford University Press, 2002.

Norwich, John Julius. *A Short Hisory of Byzantium.*
New York: Random House Vintage Books, 1997.

Rautman, Marcus. *Daily Life in the Byzantine Empire.*
Westport, Conn.: Greenwod Press, 2006.

Rosen, William. *Justinian's Flea: Plague, Empire, and the Birth of Europe.*
New York: Viking Penguin, 2007.

Treadgold, Warren. *A Concise History of Byzantium.*
New York: Palgrave, 2001.

Further Reading

Bator, Robert. *Daily Life in Ancient and Modern Istanbul.*
Minneapolis: Runestone Press, 2000.

Bowden, Rob. *Global Cities: Istanbul.*
New York: Chelsea House Publishers, 2007.

Marston, Elsa. *The Byzantine Empire.*
New York: Marshall Cavendish Benchmark Books, 2003.

Panchyk, Richard. *Archaeology for Kids: Uncovering the Mysteries of Our Past.* Chicago: Chicago Review Press, 2001.

On the Web

Use FactHound to find Internet sites related to this book. All of the sites on FactHound have been researched by our staff.

Here's all you do:
Visit *www.facthound.com*

Type in this code: 9780756545659

Titles in this Series:

The Byzantine Empire
Ancient China
Ancient Egypt
Ancient Greece
The Ancient Maya
Mesopotamia

Index

About the Author

Jenny Fretland VanVoorst is a writer and editor of books for young people. She enjoys learning about history, from the rise of the ancient Egyptians to the fall of the Soviet Union. When she's not reading and writing, VanVoorst enjoys kayaking, playing the harmonica, and watching wildlife. She lives in Minneapolis, Minnesota, with her husband, Brian, and their two pets.